HOW TO MARKET AND SELL YOUR ONLINE COURSE IN UDEMY

TIPS AND TRICKS ON MAKING MONEY TEACHING AN ONLINE COURSE

BY SMART READS

Free Audiobook

As a thank you for being a Smart Reader you can choose 2 FREE audiobooks from audible.com. Simply sign up for free by visiting www.audibletrial.com/Travis to get your books.

Visit:
www.smartreads.co/freebooks
to receive Smart Reads books for FREE

Check us out on Instagram:
www.instagram.com/smart_readers
@smart_readers

ABOUT SMARTREADS

Choose Smart Reads and get smart every time. Smart Reads sorts through all the best content and condenses the most helpful information into easily digestible chunks.

We design our books to be short, easy to read and highly informative. Leaving you with maximum understanding in the least amount of time.

Smart Reads aims to accelerate the spread of quality information so we've taken the copyright off everything we publish and donate our material directly to the public domain. You can read our uncopyright below.

We believe in paying it forward and donate 5% of our net sales to Pencils of Promise to build schools, train teachers and support child education.

To limit our footprint and restore forests around the globe we are planting a tree for every 10 hardcover books we sell.

Thanks for choosing Smart Reads and helping us help the planet.

Sincerely,

Travis & the Smart Reads Team

INTRODUCTION

Okay, so you've got a great course on your hands. You don't need me to tell you how great it is. You know how great it is. But how are you and your great course going to stand out in this world of 7,000,000,000 people? How are people going to notice you above the established stars of social media?

YOU don't have 50,000,000 people following you on twitter, and neither do you have the marketing budget of the Super Bowl.

Apologies for the tough love, but I need to ask you once again - WHO are YOU?

Whether you like to hear it or not, the answer is, you're nobody. And if you want to turn your course into a success, you must start with the acceptance that you are nobody who needs to stop looking wistfully at passive income as something that's going to change your life around forever in just a few days.

It's time to check your goals and start to seriously thinking about what it's really going to take to get your course on Udemy's bestseller's list.

TABLE OF CONTENTS

Your family and friends have likely promised you they'll purchase the course. While that's always good, your aim is to sell your course to thousands of students worldwide.

That sounds like a lot, but now is the time to be bold, brave and confident. Passive income is derived from volume, and the more people who are aware of your course; the more chances you have of selling it to more people.

Remember: More + More = More

Being Successful on Udemy boils down to mastering six things:

1.) Topic selection
2.) Unique Value Proposition
3.) Quality of your Content
4.) Pricing Strategy
5.) Social Proofing
6.) Marketing

CHAPTER 1: MAKE MARKETING YOUR NUMBER ONE PRIORITY

If you want to make enough money from passive income so you can not only pay the bills but also enjoy financial freedom, your main task should be to get good at marketing. In other words, you need to become a marketing master.

Sounds daunting? It isn't! And the best part is that good marketing doesn't mean having to spend thousands and thousands of dollars. In fact, most of the best marketing tactics can be done for free.

But it's important to remember that marketing is time-consuming. It isn't something you can do once and expect that to be that. It's something you have to keep returning to again and again until you start to achieve the results you want. What's more, certain marketing strategies don't always work straight off the bat. Sometimes, they need to be tweaked.

But if you keep at it, marketing gets results. It helps you to stand out in a very saturated market and for this reason alone you have to start making it your number one priority. If you're not good at marketing, it's going to be a HUGE problem. It's going to prevent

your products or services from ever selling more than a handful each week.

Perhaps you've got a friend who's written an excellent novel and tried to sell it on Amazon Kindle. They were super excited to price it up and start selling, and so were you. You genuinely believed this was a fine novel that was going to sell well. Unfortunately, it didn't. Sales were okay at first, but leveled off after a week and dropped off altogether after a month. Your friend lost confidence and you rail against the system.

"How come all these crummy books are selling so well when my friends great book isn't selling at all?"

The reason is simple: Your friend may be a fine storyteller, but likely not a good marketer.

To sell online, you have to be good at whatever craft you've chosen, but you have to be even better at marketing.

So many people (especially artists) fail to get this. They think talent alone is enough to get them noticed on the Internet. As unfair as it may seem, it isn't.

Marketing is what you need to do to raise awareness of what you are selling. You market your products in such a way that you are telling people what kind of value your products will add to their lives, and how it will make them feel. People may not buy it - but at least they're aware that it exists.

There are four "P's" in each marketing strategy:

1.) Product
2.) Promotion
3.) Price
4.) Place

As an instructor, you only need to manage the second and third ones, since one and two should already be sorted.

CHAPTER 2: THE DIFFERENT TYPES OF MARKETING

Pull vs. Push Marketing

Push and pull are the two types of marketing activities you need to know. The key difference between the two is how they are used to approach consumers.

If you utilize push marketing, it's normal to effectively push your products onto potential buyers. Let's say, for example, that you add a link to your course on your social media profile. This is known as a push marketing technique.

When you use push marketing, you are pushing the course to your audience or buyers. Meanwhile, in pull marketing, you are hoping that people will somehow find their way to you and your course.

Pull marketing is trickier compared to push marketing. By itself, it isn't enough to drive sales, as the competition is just too stiff. Push marketing, however, is much more forceful as you're actively barging your way into the marketplace past distractions. You're catching the attention of people.

Here are a few examples of push marketing strategies:

1.) You fire off emails to people in your network, letting them know about your new course.
2.) You launch a contest on social media, with the winner getting a free copy of your course.
3.) You promote a brand new course to students who bought the first one.

Here are a few examples of pull marketing:

1.) You launch a contest and issue a press release about it.
2.) You run a Google AdWords campaign.
3.) You write a blog post about your course.

Automated vs. Active vs. Passive Marketing
There are other key concepts in marketing you should also be aware of. These include automated, passive, and active marketing.

Passive and active approaches are similar to pull and push marketing. Automated is another key marketing concept that is effectively an amalgamation of both the passive and active approach.

Active marketing is similar to push marketing in the sense that you as a marketer assume an active role as you set about promoting your course. As an example, you may promote a contest to your email subscribers.

Passive marketing is more closely related to pull marketing in the sense that you as a marketer adopt a more passive role to promote your course. An example of the passive marketing approach would be when you rely on affiliates or Udemy itself to market the course.

Most marketing strategies make use of both passive and active approaches. However, it's essential that you have an active mindset at all times. Why? Because this will give you the winner's edge, allowing you to stand out from your competitors.

It's all about being assertive and taking control. Like with anything in life, if you remain passive, you remain in the shadows. You might be moderately successful, but you're hardly going to achieve success on the same level as someone who has taken active participation. You need to take control of your marketing. Actively work on it each day, using your passive activities to support your ability to be seen.

But what happens when you simply haven't got the time to actively market your course?

Many people are very good at creating the product - whether it's an online course or an e-book - but when it comes time to market the product, all of a sudden they have no time. However, if you really don't have the time to devote to marketing your product, you can turn to automated marketing.

Automated marketing combines all the marketing concepts covered so far:

• Pull
• Push
• Passive
• Active

It rolls them all into one.

For automated marketing, you can turn to platforms like Bugger, Friends + Me and HootSuite to preschedule your promotional posts in a way that they're running all the time for you.

If you go this route, make sure to consistently check your click counts to monitor how many more people are aware that you and your product exists. It's a great feeling to know that you're reaching thousands more people. Plus, it's really easy to do.

The best thing about these automated promotional posts is that they take care of themselves while you're free to focus on what matters - developing more courses, refining the ones you've already made, or pursuing other goals.

There are of course, a few things you need to remember when doing automated marketing:

Always remember that nobody wants to be hammered by your posts. They don't want you to bombard them with promotional posts constantly. Posting every 15 minutes is harmful to your brand, and it will cause people to unfollow you.

Twitter is the only place where you can get away with promoting the same course over and over again with great frequency because it's essentially a live feed that is updating constantly. As such, it certainly isn't a given that a follower will come across the same promotional post every time you re-post it.

Facebook is different. If you promote your course every 15 minutes, people will notice and they'll get annoyed and likely unfollow you.

When it comes to timeframes, you can get away with posting every 15 minutes on Twitter but on other social media platforms like Facebook and LinkedIn, it's best to limit your posting to twice a day. Any more than that and you could annoy a lot of people and become known as "that annoying brand."

Remember, people by and large use Facebook to connect with friends. The last thing they want is for you to be in their faces all the time with your "Hey! Look at me and my brand new course!"

The thing is, you likely won't catch someone's attention the first time they come across your promotional post on Facebook. They'll notice you and they might become curious. But they might not click or even buy. This is fine, because there's still time. Post the same thing again the next day, and maybe they'll see it again. If they don't act then it's still not a problem.

Eventually, you might catch them on a day when they finally think, "Hmm, this course keeps popping up on my feed. I'm going to check it out." And bingo! You've got them.

Remember, if you bombard them, they'll likely go away and escape from you. Then you won't have any potential audience at all. Always play it cool. Take your time. Be sensible and be polite. Don't be intrusive of anybody's time because nobody likes that, especially not on their Facebook.

On Twitter, a lot of entrepreneurs have two accounts. One is for their main audience while the other is for automated posts or marketing. You can do this as well to ensure your main audience won't get peeved at you posting and reposting every few minutes. Just make sure to also share the info to your main audience so they know you actually have a course they can purchase.

CHAPTER 3: SCRUTINIZING YOUR MARKETING ACTIVITIES

There are two key obstacles that marketers have traditionally found hard to overcome for years:

1.) The subjective nature of marketing.
2.) The fact that it isn't always easy to quantify your marketing efforts - basically, you don't always know when something is working and when it isn't.

However, such challenges beset the offline marketing world. The online world of marketing is more resistant to these problems because it has the antidote in the form of tools, including Google Analytics.

All you need to do is open up a Google Analytics account to check how well your marketing efforts are working (or how well they aren't working!)

Google Analytics is just the tip of the iceberg - there are MANY online tools and platforms that can help you understand your marketing efforts and their potency. These tools include the popular KissMetrics, as well as MailPoet. WordPress also has other tools you can use.

Gauging the effectiveness of a website's performance is one thing, but you want to gauge how well your

Udemy marketing strategies are performing. And guess what, you can do that, too!

Udemy allows you to create your own coupon codes, as well as name them. You can then link these coupon codes to your promotional and marketing activities. As an example, imagine you've decided to run a holiday promotion. Your coupon could read something like XMAS17XX, which helps you track how well that promotion is performing, and how many sales it's bringing home.

On Twitter, you'd use a code like TWIT17XX in order to track the sales that are coming from your Twitter profile. If you name your conventions, you can more easily keep track of and manage your sales and promotions, so that you know what's working and what's not working.

If it were granular info that you want more of, you'd be better off ignoring Conversion Analytics, which comes with Udemy. Instead, open up an account with Google Analytics (it's free). It's a much better and easier way of tracking everything, from bounce rates to sales conversions to page visits.

Setting up a Google Analytics account is easy, but you might need a bit of help getting the hang of things. If so, there are plenty of helpful tools (including blogs) that will help on this end, while Google provides a tutorial.

If you try Google Analytics (or have tried it in the past) and find that it's too much hassle for you, you might want to give Bitly.com a shot. It's simpler than Google Analytics, if a bit less in-depth. However, it's a great tool for tracking your clicks, as well as finding out where those clicks come from. What's more, it's helpful when shortening URLS so you can easily automate posts. It essentially speeds up the posting process.

With Bitly.com, you can also customize any BitLinks so you're essentially customizing your marketing strategy in a way that suits you and your target audience better.

Of course, it's crucial to remember that while knowing your marketing analytics and where your buyers are coming from is a good idea, you shouldn't spend too much time frying your brain over it all. It doesn't need to be that complicated. What you're looking for is what works and what doesn't. And that's it. You can then double down on what's working while tweaking or abandoning what isn't working. It's that simple.

But without an analytics tool, you simply won't have the knowledge to know where you're going right and wrong.

While it's true, there are people who don't use an analytics tool at all, instead, they rely purely on intuition. While this is admirable, these people are natural born mavericks who have an eye for this sort of thing. Chances are, most of you won't be like this and would benefit greatly from knowing how to use and understand the results churned out by analytics.

The key takeaway is that you need to do whatever it takes so you don't get stuck using the same ineffective marketing strategy over and over and over again.

It's like Albert Einstein said, "Insanity is doing the same thing over and over again and expecting different results."

CHAPTER 4: DOING MARKET RESEARCH

What is market research? Put simply, it's when you gather, analyze and interpret info about a specific market, as well as the service or product you're thinking of offering in the said market.

You'll want to take a close look at potential customers to see if this is something they want, as well as past mistakes made by other companies who have tried to sell this before but without much success. You'll need to delve into the spending habits of consumers, as well as their needs. Find out if they've got a problem that needs solving, as well as whether there is a gap in the market for the product you've got. Also make sure to check out competitors to see what they're selling, and whether or not your product or service is much different.

When you're delivering a course, there are some questions you'll need to ask about your potential customers or students:

1.) What is their age range?
2.) Where are they living?
3.) What language are they speaking?
4.) What is their main language?

5.) Is their ethnic background important for this course?

6.) How educated are they? Do they have a degree? Do they need one?

7.) How much time are they spending on the Internet?

8.) Do they love to learn?

9.) Do they often buy online courses?

10.) Is this their first time buying a course?

11.) Would they be likely to study your subject online, or would they do it offline?

12.) What would need to happen for them to enroll?

13.) Are your competitors better than you?

14.) Do they need more incentives to study online?

15.) Are they active on social media?

16.) How much time are they spending on social media?

17.) Are they active most in the morning, afternoon, evening or late at night?

These are just a handful of questions that can give you better insight into who you're targeting, and what their needs and wants are. You might be able to answer some of the questions with precision, but for others you might need to fill in the gaps with a bit of guessing. The key takeaway is you learn more about who you're trying to sell to so that you have a better chance of selling!

Market research is all about gaining knowledge about a market and then using it. Keep in mind that market research can be a total waste of time if you gain knowledge but then don't use it. If you've ever seen the reality TV show The Apprentice, you'll have seen contestants countless times carrying out market research, only to then go against it all. The host can then be seen tearing his hair out at this madness!

Whatever your market research tells you about a market, make sure to take it as truth. Why? Because it IS the truth. Don't ignore it or try to shape a new narrative about the market by interpreting data in a different way. That's a surefire way of failing and misjudging your market.

CHAPTER 5: CHOOSING YOUR MARKETING CHANNELS

There are so many marketing channels available for you to use. They exist both offline and online. For the moment, you don't really need to pay too much attention to offline marketing strategies. Maybe if you go to a networking event or a conference, you could put in a bit of effort. For now, all your effort should be directed at online marketing channels. Why? Because online services and products sell better when the marketing efforts are online-based. It's basic math.

Here are a few online channel suggestions:

• Udemy
• A website for your course
• Email
• Blogs
• Social media
• Podcasts
• Video
• Live videos
• Newsletters
• Online forums
• Paid ads
• Paid banners

And here are some of offline channels you may want to consider when it suits you:

- Print
- Direct mail
- Telemarketing
- Television
- Radio
- Conferences and events
- Networking marketing
- Billboards
- Press releases
- Text messaging

As you can imagine, offline channels would require a bigger effort from you, and the results are not guaranteed to be as good as the ones produced by your online marketing efforts.

How Big Is Your Footprint on Social Media?
Let's talk about your footprint on social media. How big is it? Have you been making one?

Your online footprint is basically a collation of your data that you've left behind in the same way a snail leaves behind its slime. When you've been active on social media, there is often a clue you've left behind about yourself that others use to put together a profile about you. For example, you tweet on Twitter, post updates on Facebook and leave selfies everywhere.

This is your online footprint, and people are using it to gather information about you and decide what you're all about. Essentially, it's your brand you're building as you roam around social media. And if you're trying to sell a course, you must give off the impression that you're an expert in your field who knows what you're talking about. You need to look professional and smart.

The last thing you want is for a potential student to look you up on Google, only to find a questionable post you wrote about how much you hate students on the first page!

Hopefully that won't ever happen, but the point is that your online footprint needs to show how credible you are. Think of it as an aid to all your marketing efforts. If a student Google's you and forms an impression of a warm, successful expert in their field who has released books on the subject and has many testimonials, they are more likely to buy your course than if they Googled you and found no trace except a dodgy photo from 2008.

The point is that you should spend a bit of time working on your online footprint. Blog on LinkedIn or maybe do a guest post. Get yourself a professional Facebook page and smarten up your Twitter. Polish your website and make sure it's up date. Show off your expertise because it's almost a guarantee that your potential students will Google you.

Keep Googling yourself to see how you look. If you come across things you don't want to see, find out if there is a way you can contact whoever is in charge of the website and kindly ask them if they can remove it.

The main thing is that you need to be consistent. Most people tend to avoid those who are inconsistent and prefer individuals who are consistent, both with their beliefs and attitudes.

Also, if you've written e-Books in the past and sold them on Amazon, consider removing them if they're struggling with bad reviews. To sell your course you need leverage. Remove anything that is damaging your brand and credibility. Other things you need to tidy up are your photographs. What students are looking for are professional headshots of yourself. If all they find are tiny-sized images of you playing beer pong, they're hardly going to be convinced you're the right tutor for them. Fix up your images across your social media platforms.

The main thing is that you're consistent. Customers trust brands and people that are consistent. This means being consistent with your actions and behavior, as well as your personal branding.

Here are a few things to take care of on your social media profiles:

1.) Make sure you have a good quality, professional headshot. If possible, pay a pro photographer to take a few photographs of you, choose the best one and upload it.
2.) Include a short bio (no more than 150 words but preferably even less than that.)
3.) Include three to four VERY SHORT paragraphs of info about yourself and what you do.
4.) Make sure your introduction captures people's attention. Maybe start with a question that highlights a problem your students might have.
5.) Reserve two or three lines that highlight your expertise and background. You're selling a course, so use your background as leverage. It will give you credibility and raise your level of expertise.
6.) Publish relevant content on the Internet like on blogs and include links to your course.

You may be unsure at this point about which websites and platforms you need to be on. This will depend on your needs and something you need to figure out from the onset. When you're weighing your options, ask yourself a few questions:

1.) What value proposition does the website have?
2.) How will this website help me to produce income?
3.) Is the website getting more popular or less popular? Is it on the way up, or is it on the way down?
4.) How many people visit it each month? What's the traffic like?
5.) Does the site look visually appealing? Does the company put effort into maintaining it?
6.) How high is the user engagement?
7.) Will I need to be really active if I want to get the best results?
8.) Are the people who visit the site the type of people who will buy my course? Does the website target audience that match up with mine?

Lastly, there is usually one powerful platform where you will focus 70% of your time. This website needs to be worth it. Identify which is going to be your biggest winner.

CHAPTER 6: MAKING YOUR COURSE MARKETABLE

Remember Blackberry? They really looked like they were going places in the Smartphone market. Then one day they just disappeared. What happened to them? Apple smashed them. How? By being better than them.

Apple didn't even have to try too hard. Apple just did what Apple has been doing for years now. They produced stylish, innovative, sleek and modern products.

Blackberry, on the other hand, was struggling with products that folks were starting to perceive as being dull and behind the times. They had quickly gone out of fashion. No one was buying anymore, not when they could buy a slick Apple product.

This is a key point: Your course has to be awesome and current. If it isn't, even the world's greatest ever marketers can't help you. You can't sell a dead horse.

There are a lot of would-be online tutors who dive into their marketing strategies without properly questioning whether or not their course is even marketable. You have to make your product desirable and filled with value for your students. If you market a bad product really well, it might sell based on your marketing strengths alone. But rest assured, it will be returned and the customers will leave bad reviews. And then you'll really have nowhere to go. Your brand will be ruined and your reputation and credibility will be in tatters.

Before you start marketing your course, first make sure it is actually marketable. When you sell a marketable course that people enjoy and get a lot of satisfaction out of, customers will start leaving you positive reviews, which boosts your courses marketability and desirability even more.

When making sure that your course is marketable, here are a few things to consider:

1,) Is your title captivating? Does it grab our attention? Does it make us want to take a peek inside?

2.) Does your subtitle deliver on the promise of your title by tantalizing us even more? Have you addressed a problem that your students have while also guaranteeing that you're going to solve it?

3.) What is your course image like? Is it bland? Is it formal and does it smack of the lifeless images people used to see as kids in school textbooks? Or is it empowering and exiting? Does it inspire students to want to learn from you?

4.) Also make sure you have a promo video. Why? Because everyone loves a video! Your video must be short (no longer than two minutes), informative, engaging and even entertaining. Cover all the benefits that your course will bring, and include a call to action at the end. If you're presenting the video, be energetic and excited.

For inspiration, watch similar videos. Remember, this is all about your students. Don't make this video about you and how awesome you are as a teacher. As consumers, all they want to know is what's in it for them. So tell them!

5.) Include a course description that covers what your course is about. If writing is not your forte, it's a good idea to hire a copywriter for this bit. If your description is weak, it's going to sabotage your best marketing efforts.

6.) Label each lecture. Customers are good at quickly scanning through text. Give them snappy lecture titles that briefly but powerfully sum up what each lesson is about so they know instantly that this is the right course for them.

7.) Reviews! Reviews are your references. Buyers look at reviews to get an idea of your credentials. The more good reviews your course has, the more credible it looks.

It's really hard to sell a course that has only one or two reviews. So you need to get at least TEN before you can start seriously selling.

CHAPTER 7: GETTING READY TO LAUNCH

Eventually, your course will be available to download on Udemy. This will be an exciting date for you, and no doubt one that you pen into your calendar before it arrives. But this date is not the same date as the one for your promotional launch. This is a different date that you control, and as such it's one that you orchestrate and decide on.

Expert marketers will set the date for their promotional launch about a week after their course has gone live - not before. Doing this will boost awareness of the course.

Before launching the course, you'll need to first make sure it's primed to be marketed. You will also need to find ways of getting students to enroll as soon as possible before you promote your course. The easiest and no doubt best way to do this is to make it available for free, and push/pull it on FB via the numerous Udemy groups that are on there.

Just quickly, it's worth mentioning that during the holidays people tend not to pay much attention to promotion. We call this the holiday blackout when people are too busy doing other things - such as Christmas and the New Year. However, students are always interested, and even more so at this time of the year (usually when they realize how much money they've spent and therefore could do with a bargain!)

When you launch your course, you need to get yourself involved in some push marketing strategies. You need to be active and get on the rooftop, letting people know that you've got a course.

Here are some things to take into consideration for your launch:

1.) What type of promotions are you considering? A discount or maybe a giveaway?
2.) How many days before the launch will you start to promote?
3.) Which channels are you going to use for promotion?
4.) Are you going to get some class content written down, perhaps on a blog post, that you and others can share?
5.) Maybe you've got other courses that you can now use to leverage announcements regarding your new course?
6.) How are you going to use your followers and subscribers to help you spread the word about your course?

7.) Are there any online groups and websites you can leverage?

8.) Maybe there are some influencers (especially on LinkedIn) who can help you with your promotional activities?

9.) How much is all this going to cost you? (Clue - it shouldn't cost you much!)

10.) What strategies are you going to employ so that your launch boosts your email marketing list?

11.) What automated marketing efforts are you going to run along with your push marketing strategies?

12.) How are you going to keep track of the launch? How will you find out how successful or unsuccessful it's been?

There is certainly no universal, objective, surefire methods of launching a course. What worked for one person might not work for you. This is why it's important to find out the answers to this question so you have a better understanding of what type of marketing you'll need for your course. Use the questions to fire your creativity. Let them help you form some ideas.

A marketing plan outlines your goals, timelines, priorities, and activities. It should be simple, and should look a little bit something like this:

ACTIVITY: On Monday I will post something to my blog.

TIMELINE: I will post something to my blog each and every Monday.

GOAL: My aim with my blog is to reach a wider audience.

You could make blog posting your top priority, and at the end of every quarter, you could measure your traffic to see how successful your blog posts have been. If you're presently working on an online marketing plan, you could tweak it so that it incorporates your promotional work.

If, on the other hand, you don't have a marketing plan, you should definitely think about creating a brief document (it doesn't have to be more than two pages) that outlines your plans and subsequent activities. Remember to keep your plan simple, as it will be a lot easier to keep track of and dedicate yourself to. Kick things off with two or three activities, before adding to them as you go along.

You need to be wary of duplication. It can be really easy to get sucked into the trap of creating activities that are similar. Create ones that are distinct enough so that they're not mere duplications, as this will only begin to slow down the effectiveness of your marketing activities.

It's important that you put as much time and energy behind each activity. The more effort you put into creating content, for example, the more people will sit up and take notice of it.

People are very good at gauging good quality content, and they're very good at responding to it. They might, for example, comment on it, or even share it (which would be awesome.)

If people are not actively engaging and interacting with your content, it means there is either a problem with your marketing plan, or it means that you're simply not putting enough time and energy into your efforts.

CHAPTER 8: ONLINE MARKETING TACTICS

We can break online marketing tactics into 6 groups. These are:

1.) Video Marketing
2.) Social Media Marketing
3.) Email Marketing
4.) Search Marketing
5.) Content Marketing
6.) Paid Advertising

Some of these activities are made up of push marketing techniques, while others are made up of pull marketing techniques.

Video Marketing is all about creating short, snappy videos, posting them online and hoping that people share them.

Lots of marketers today are using YouTube to inform consumers about their services and products. Online videos are really popular right now, primarily because of the visual culture the world is not in. People just love to see a big PLAY button, and they love to watch a friendly, personable guy or girl convey cool, useful information to them.

Social Media Marketing is often used to boost website traffic, sales and general attention via social media sites, like Google +, Facebook, LinkedIn and Twitter. People who market on social media focus their efforts on getting people to read their posts but, more importantly, to also share them.

Email marketing is a type of marketing that is - you guessed it - email-based. We use emails to send out newsletters, campaigns and sales letters. If you have noticed, many websites you visit now prompt you to subscribe just seconds after you've landed on their page. While this can seem like an invasive tactic, it does work and it's a great way to build your email list. And as any online marketer will tell you, email marketing is now just as relevant as ever.

What about search marketing? This type of marketing involves using search engines to grow your traffic. You employ both unpaid and paid marketing efforts to this end. What would you pay for? You would pay for add placements which are centered on keywords.

What would you not pay for? You wouldn't pay for SEO (unless you hire an SEO person.) SEO means search engine optimization. Essentially, your content contains keywords that Internet users are searching for in Google. If you have the keywords they're looking for, there's a good chance they'll find your website.

Content marketing is pretty self-explanatory - it's basically having good, relevant content. The types of content include video content, blog posts, podcasts, info graphics and images. It's all kinds of stuff and people and Google love to see you post new content regularly.

Your content has to be pretty to look at, but for it to be effective it also needs to contain a call to action. Essentially, at the end of your video or blog post, there should be a call to your reader/watcher/listener to go and do something. Maybe you want them to subscribe or buy your course.

You have to be direct with your call to action; otherwise they just won't do what you want them to do. Want them to subscribe? Then tell them!

Lastly, paid advertising is a failsafe tactic that is pretty much guaranteed to work. You pay for ads, target them at the right audience, people see those ads, and come over to see what you've got. Paid advertising is an easy way of making people aware of your course.

So which approach works the best? It depends on a few variables. Each tactic has its set of pros and cons, and the ones you choose to use should depend on what your market is, as well as the type of course you've got.

The best thing is to dabble with each tactic, as this is a good way to enhance your core promotional strategy. Spend some time experimenting with different tactics. Find out which ones work for you and which ones don't. Analyze your activities every three months so you don't end up spending a whole year on a strategy that isn't even working.

CHAPTER 9: MARKETING EFFORTS

Type "online marketing efforts" into Google and you'll find lots of things to include in your own marketing strategy. Among these are some tried and tested strategies that people before you have already used, and which you should definitely consider using, too.

Some of these efforts will help you make yourself and your course more discoverable, and this is important. How easy are you to find on the Internet? When people Google your name, do you pop up on page one, or is page one instead flooded with information about a photographer with the exact same name as you?

What is the first page directly related to you that pops up? Is it your courses website or your LinkedIn profile? Or is it a regrettable eBook you tried selling two years ago that no one bought?

You need to have strong online presence. You need to be discoverable. A lot of marketing efforts are about making people aware of you as they are about making people aware of your course. The two really go hand in hand - as they should. If you're going to be spending money on someone's course, you want to know what their credentials are. If you can't find anything on the

Internet about them, it's going to undermine your confidence in them.

Video Marketing Efforts

Firstly, you need to build a YouTube following. You need to have a presence on this channel. YouTube, like Udemy, is a video platform. Therefore, it makes sense that you add video marketing to your marketing efforts. You can use YouTube as the perfect weapon to drive more traffic to your Udemy course.

YouTube, after all, is the most popular video platform on the Internet - by a long way. Billions of new views are registered each and every day, and until you get yourself registered on this channel, you're just losing out.

One way you could market yourself on YouTube is by recording and uploading a lecture. This is easy to do. After all, this is your market! All you need to do is give a short lecture in something related to your course, add a relevant title, include some keywords in the description, and get it uploaded.

At the end of the video, include a call to action. This is the most important bit! Don't forget it.

Develop Some New Courses

If you've already got some courses under your belt, now is the time to leverage them. This is a fantastic way of marketing your new course, and it's also really easy. After all, you've already got the material.

When Udemy was first launched, it quickly became a bit of an unspoken agreement by all that having success with your first course was enough to make your second course a success, too. However, things have changed since those early days. There are now way more courses on Udemy than there was back then, which means that if you want to create sustainable income (and much more than that), you can't rely on one course alone. You instead need to create three or even six courses.

This sounds like a lot, but if you listen to e-book writers, they will tell you that they're currently selling ten or more e-Books online - all at the same time. They know that to make a good living out of this, the trick is to launch as many quality products as possible.

As a lecturer, it's easy for you to leverage your existing course content. You can use one course to promote another related one, and vice versa. The more courses you have, the more you can use your other courses and lectures to promote them.

Adding Fresh Content To Your Course

When you add fresh content to the course, it keeps your course visible. It also shows that you care about your course enough to return to it and tweak the bits that aren't working. Students will notice this, and they will happily leave you good reviews and recommend the course to others. You should look to add at least one new discussion related to your course each month. This will keep it fresh, and ensure that it stays relevant.

Going Live

Live video. How do you feel about that? For some, the idea of a live video is nerve wracking. But it's something that you should start to explore as part of your video marketing activities.

You can use AnyMeeting and Google + Hangouts to easily arrange a live event. Your live event can be studiously planned in advance, or it can be totally spontaneous. How sweet is it when we're just milling around on Facebook and our favorite lecturer pops up with a live video? It's a nice surprise.

Your live video can be a standalone piece, or it could be a part of a series. For example, perhaps you want to have Teachers Corner every Monday (or something that sounds a LOT less corny.)

Live videos are a fantastic way of interacting with your followers, and you get to read feedback in real time. Live video also enhances your appeal, and shows that you're authentic. You're prepared to take some time out of your schedule to interact with your followers, answering their questions and reading out their comments.

Try not to use live video as way to promote your course. Instead, you should see it as a chance to talk about aspects of the course, or hand out tips. At the end of the video, you could include a call to action, such as "you can catch me over at Udemy."

Slot Videos Into Your Social Media
More and more people are adding videos to their Twitter profile. It's really easy to do and doesn't take much time at all. And it's time for you to start doing it too as it will boost engagement.

Go To Events - And Present!
Live video is one thing. But how do you fancy presenting at a conference and networking events?

This is an offline marketing activity. While networking events are a good way of meeting new people, they're not really an effective way of promoting your course - unless you get up and address every one in the room.

It's likely that if you present at a conference or networking event you're the only Udemy lecturer in the room. This gives you an advantage. You should also arrange to have someone record your presentation, so that you can then upload it to your website, as well as your YouTube channel.

Social Media Efforts
Here is a checklist of things you need to take into consideration when you market yourself and your course on social media:

• Make sure that all your profiles are complete and optimized (a half-finished profile is a major turn-off and you'll lose all credibility.)
• Add the right links so that you can direct the traffic.
• Post frequently, both via automation and in real time.
• Always include hash tags, and don't forget to jump onto trending hash tags. If possible, spot a hash tag before it trends and be one of the first to use it.
• Reply to messages and comments. Who knows where they could take you?

• Do not post spammy content. No one appreciates it.
• If you put a lot of time and effort into this, the results will come.

Your Twitter Profile

Here are a few ways you can enhance your twitter profile:

• If someone from your domain follows you, be gracious enough to follow back. It could lead to something.
• Similarly, if someone from your domain sends you a message or responds to a tweet, reply to them.
• Each time someone new follows you, send them an automated message
• Use vanity links for more traffic.
• Pin a post - make sure this post is useful to others, and also drives them to your course.

Your Facebook Profile:

Here are a few ways you can enhance your Facebook profile:

• Make a brand page or a product page that isn't the same as your personal, social profile.
• Pin a post - make sure this post is useful to others, eye-catching, and also drives them to your course.

Your LinkedIn Profile:
Here are a few ways you can enhance your LinkedIn profile:

• Use the platforms' blog feature to post articles and announcements.
• Highlight course content with the SlideShare app.
• Establish contact with fellow LinkedIn users who are in the same domain as you. See what they can do for you, and what you can do for them.
• Join groups that are relevant to your course and be active in them. Comment, post, interact. Get to know people and make your presence felt.

Join Facebook Groups
There are so many Facebook groups on Facebook, and there will be some communities that are relevant to your course, and which are therefore worth your time joining and contributing to.

To find them, search for Udemy and see what comes up. They won't all be fantastic, so you may have to do a bit of research to weed out the worst ones and focus on the best. Once you're in the group, make sure that you're active. Let people know who you are and what your course is all about. Flaunt your skills by offering tips and advice. Don't join a group to selfishly take what you can from it. Help others.

Contribution makes you feel good, but it also casts you in a positive light with others. They'll see that you've got something valuable to offer, and that you're not purely in it for yourself.

Create You Own Group
The leaders in a particular field don't tend to just join groups created by others - they go ahead and create groups themselves. This gives you enormous presence. It helps to build your brand, establish your authority in a particular field, grow your list of important contacts and of course, boost your sales.

We're all attracted to leaders. In fact, we're so attracted to leaders in a group that we click their profile and learn more about them. Maybe we'll even add them as a friend. You can use your group to offer tips and advice, as well as promote your free courses, if you have any.

Remember, people love free things. Tim Ferris once said that by and large, he gives away MOST of his stuff for free. The only thing he sells for cash are the premium stuff, which he knows, will make him a lot of money in one go.

Make Sure That Your Promotional Posts Are Automated

If you spend $9 on anything this month, I suggest that you spend it on HootSuite. HootSuite is known to elite marketers - and that's basically it. Everyone else who is struggling in vain to market their course aren't aware of HootSuite's value - and that's a real shame.

HootSuite costs just $9 per month. It lets you upload your posts in bulk and preschedule them so you never have to wake up in the morning realizing you forgot to publish your weekly blog post last night ever again. In other words, it takes a massive load off. By "bulk" uploading, it doesn't mean five or ten posts. It doesn't even mean 100 posts. Nope. I mean up to three-hundred and fifty posts!

Basically, you're putting rocket fuel into your social media marketing efforts if you pay just $9 per month for Hoot Suite. There is a 30 day free trial offered just in case you're not sure.

Now, uploading three hundred and fifty posts sounds complex - and it sort of is. To get a lid on your system, you will need to do a bit of experimenting. You won't get it right the first time around. However, once you get into the swing of things (and you soon will do), you'll realize that HS is basically magic. Pretty soon, you will be able to schedule around seven hundred posts.

It's important to start small, though. Begin with around fifty prescheduled posts before building up.

If you do decide to give HootSuite a shot, here are some things to bar in mind:

1.) You can't preschedule any more than three hundred and fifty posts at any one time. To prevent uploads from overlapping in the future (trust me, this can easily happen), it's best to avoid doing the full three-hundred and fifty and instead start small.

2.) Don't duplicate your post. This is banned and will land you in hot water as doing so will be violating the terms and conditions. You don't want to get violated for this.

3.) Twitter only as 140 characters for each tweet, which is a bit restrictive. There is a way around this, though, and that's by shortening your links with Owl.ly or Bit.ly before attaching to the CSV file.

4.) You can't upload an MS Excel file. It needs to be a CSV file. However, they look pretty much the same.

5.) Bulk uploading is good, but it has one drawback - it doesn't let you add images. It's not a massive inconvenience, though, as you can just add them to you real time posts instead. Bingo.

6.) Don't schedule your posts two minutes into the future - it's too close. Schedule them at least 10 minutes before just to be safe.

7.) HootSuite is very good at rounding up odd numbers. As such, you must make sure that your post times end with a 0 or a 5. Examples - 12:15 and 13:00

Email Marketing
Let's now focus on email marketing. Despite what you may have been told, email is still alive and kicking. Social media, as many predicted hasn't destroyed it. In fact, it's probably stronger than ever. Everyone still emails, and most people check their e-mails at least once a day.

We'll begin by...

Building Your Email List

For you right now, it's vital that you have an email list. If you don't have one, you should start building one after finishing this book. This should be at the very top of your to-do list.

You can pop over to Amazon.com to find out more about the kind of resources you need to build your emailing list. There will, of course, be people who subscribe voluntarily to your email list, and these are people who are genuinely interested in you and your course. These are good, valuable customers to you because they have a genuine desire to hear all about your latest promotions and products, and how it will benefit them.

It's important that you don't view your emailing list as a competition. You don't want to see how many discounts you can offer each week, and nor do you want to email them every single day about a new promotion or offer. Indeed, the best thing to do is email your list once or twice a month. Anymore than that can seem spammy, and it can start to annoy your subscribers. If they're receiving too many emails from you, they might be inclined to click the "unsubscribe" button.

When it comes time to email your list, it's best to either make the email about a new product launch you are preparing - or one that someone you know is preparing. Naturally, subscribers need incentivizing. They need a reason to subscribe, and to keep following you.

To do this, you can offer them a discount when they subscribe to your list. The discount could apply to a course, or it could apply to a short e-book, or just some great info. Offer a coupon code and a discount to incentivize them to take action and sign up.

Run Regular Promotions
Run a promotion at least once a month. Any more than that and you and your emails could get annoying. Any less than that, and you could be losing out on making more sales and growing your customer base.

For one reason or another, a customer's interest is piqued by discounts more than it is by what we call value propositions. Udemy will offer discounts now and then, but when they don't, it's time for you to step forward and offer one.

You don't have to just run a promotion on the same day each month. There's nothing wrong with running random discounts of up to 90%. For these random discounts, you don't have to do too much planning.

You can announce the discount quite literally just a day before it takes effect.

Run A Marketing Campaign Every Quarter
Promotional discounts are one thing, but what about marketing campaigns? Marketing campaigns are harder to pull off because they require a bit more creativity on your part.

A promotion could include "tell a buddy," but marketing campaigns offer more excitement than a discount ever could - especially when you consider that Udemy itself already offers lots of discounts.

To spark people's interest in your marketing campaign, you need to be creative and imaginative. If you personally feel good about your campaign, the consumers will feel good about it too, and will want to get on board. And if they're excited about it, there's also a good chance that they'll share it.

Content, Paid and Search Marketing Efforts

Send Out A Press Release
You've no doubt seen a press release issued by a sports team or a celebrity. Maybe you've seen the ones issued by Fortune 100. But press releases aren't just released by the big guns with lots of cash and juicy

stories to tell. They are released by anyone, including people just like you who have a course to sell.

Press releases are a great way of sharing news and stories before the said news and stories comes out in the news for real. They help create anticipation. Issuing one for your course is a fantastic way of reaching more people.

Pop Over To SlideShare And Upload A Short Presentation
You should make a portion of your course available for free over at Udemy, but you need somewhere else to post free content to potential buyers. If you've got a presentation, you can pop on over to SlideShare and upload it there.

LinkedIn owns SlideShare, which should give you an idea of how professional this resource is. And while you shouldn't upload your most precious content, you should at least give enough of a sneak peek into what your course is all about so that viewers are compelled to act and buy the rest of your course. Maybe you could upload an introductory presentation that introduces the core concepts of your course, with a call to action at the end.

Write A Blog

Blogging is a great way of boosting conversions and getting your course noticed by more people. However, being a successful blogger is not easy, and it does take time to get noticed. But if you post it in the right channels - Facebook groups, your Twitter profile etc., you can start reaching more people.

The thing with blogging is that you have to write about things that people actually want to read. Don't write for yourself - write for the reader. What problems can you solve for them?

Make sure that your blog ties into your course content, and keep your topics relevant. Use SEO techniques to improve your Google rankings, and always make sure that your content is of a high quality and free from spelling mistakes and grammatical errors.

CONCLUSION

As you know by now, it's one thing to have a great course on your hands, and quite another for that course to be seen by people - and downloaded. In today's market, you have to be a hotshot marketer if you're going to make any kind on inroads with what you've got.

Marketing is all about putting in the time and making the effort, to first of all learn the techniques and then to apply them. Then, you need to track them to see what's working and what's not working, before tweaking them.

Get your marketing game on point, and your quality course will pretty much sell itself.

Good luck!

THANKS FOR READING

We really hope you enjoyed this book. If you found this material helpful feel free to share it with friends. You can also help others find it by leaving a review where you purchased the book. Your feedback will help us continue to write books you love.

The Smart Reads library is growing by the day! Make sure and check out the other wonderful books in our catalog. We would love to hear which books are your favorite.

Visit:
www.smartreads.co/freebooks
to receive Smart Reads books for FREE

Check us out on Instagram:
www.instagram.com/smart_readers
@smart_readers

Don't forget your 2 FREE audiobooks.
Use this link www.audibletrial.com/Travis to claim
your 2 FREE Books.

SMART READS ORIGINS

Smart Reads was born out of the desire to find the best information fast without having to wade through the sheer volume of fluff available online. Smart Reads combs through massive amounts of knowledge compiles the best into quick to read books on a variety of subjects.

We consider ourselves Smart Readers, not dummies. We know reading is smart. We're self taught. We like to learn a TON about a WIDE variety of topics. We have developed a love for books and we find intelligence attractive.

We found that each new topic we tried to learn about started with the challenge of finding the pieces of the puzzle that mattered most. It becomes a treasure hunt rather than an education.

Smart Reads wants to find the best of the best information for you. To condense it into a package that you can consume in an hour or less. So you can read more books about more topics in less time.

OUR MISSION

Smart Reads aims to accelerate the availability of useful information and will publish a high quality book on every major topic on amazon.

Smart Reads hopes to remove barriers to sharing by taking the copyright off everything we publish and donating it to the public domain. We hope other publishers and authors will follow our example.

Our goal is to donate $1,000,000 or more by 2020 to build over 2,000 schools by giving 5% of our net profit to Pencils of Promise.

We want to restore forests around the globe by planting a tree for every 10 physical books we sell and hope to plant over 100,000 trees by 2020.

Doesn't it feel good knowing that by educating yourself you are helping the world be a better place? We think so too...

Thanks for helping us help the world. You Smart Reader you...

Travis and the Smart Reads Team

WHY I STARTED SMART READS

Every time I wanted to learn about something new I'd have to buy 20 books on the topic and spend way too long sorting through them and reading them all until I arrived at the big picture. Until I had enough perspectives to know who was just guessing, who was uninformed and who had stumbled upon something remarkable.

I wished someone else could just go in and figure that out for me and tell me what matters. That's how smart reads was born. I want smart reads to be a company that does all that research up front. Sorts through all the content that is available on each topic and pulls out the most up to date complete understanding, then have people smarter than me package the best wisdom in an easy to understand way in the least amount of words possible.

For example, I got a new puppy so I wanted to learn about dog training. I bought 14 different books about dog training and by the time I got through the first 5 and finally started getting the big picture on the best way to train my puppy she had grown up into a dog.

Yeah she's well behaved. She doesn't poop in the house. I can get her to sit and come when I call. But what if someone else went in and read all those books for me, found the underlying themes and picked out the best information that would give me the big picture and get me right to the point. And I'd only have to read one book instead of 15.

That would be amazing. I would save time. And maybe my dog would be rolling over, cleaning up after my kids and doing the dishes by now. That my friend, is the reason I started smart reads. Because I wanted a company I can trust to deliver me the best information in an easy to understand way that I can digest in under an hour. Because dog training is one of many subjects I want to master.

The quicker I can learn a wide variety of topics the sooner that information can begin playing a role in shaping my future. And none of us knows how long that future will be. So why not do everything we can to make the best of it and consume a ton of knowledge. And I figured all the better if I can also make a positive difference in the world.

That's why we're also building schools, planting trees and challenging ideas about copyright's place in today's world. Because as a company we have to be doing everything we can to support the ecosystem that gives us all these beautiful places to read our books. Thanks for reading.

Travis

Customers Who Bought This
Customers Who Bought This Book
Also Bought

Understanding Affiliate Marketing: An Internet Marketing Guide for How To Make Money Online Using Products, Websites and Services

Blockchain Revolution: Understanding the Internet of Money

Passive Income: Do What You Want When You Want and Make Money While You Sleep

Success Principles: Techniques for Positive Thinking, Self Love and Developing a Powerful

The Everything Store Sales Guide: How to Make Money with Amazon FBA

Unlocking Potential - Master the Laws of Leadership

Reinvent Yourself: Become Instantly Likable, Captivate Anyone in Seconds and Always Know What To Say

Credit Repair Guide: How to Fix Credit Score and Remove Negatives From Credit Report